Please
date sl
by pho

www

☎ 01

100% UNOFFICIAL TRIBUTE TO THE HUNGER GAMES

A BANTAM BOOK 978 0 857 51107 2

First published in Great Britain by Bantam, an imprint of Random House Children's Books
A Random House Group Company

This edition published 2012

1 3 5 7 9 10 8 6 4 2

Picture credits: cover: BG Mikhail/andreiuc88/Shutterstock.com, BL Jeff Vespa/WireImage, BM Startraks Photo/Rex Features, BR Marcel Thomas/FilmMagic. 2: BG Roger Rosentreter/Shutterstock.com, BL gualtiero boffi/Shutterstock.com. 3: BR Valeev/Shutterstock.com. 4: BG andreiuc88/Shutterstock.com. 5: BL, BM, BR as cover. 6: see relevant pages. 7: BG EtiAmmos/Shutterstock.com. 8: BG Mary Terriberry/Shutterstock.com, TL Peter Brooker/Rex Features, ML Joe Seer/Shutterstock.com, BL Helga Esteb/Shutterstock.com. 9: BG Carlos Caetano/Shutterstock.com, TR Left Eyed Photography/Shutterstock.com, ML & BR Joe Seer/Shutterstock.com. 10: BG andreiuc88/Shutterstock.com, ML ©Hallmark/Everett/Rex Feature, BL Joe Seer/Shutterstock.com, M keellla/Shutterstock.com. 11: M Donna Ward/Getty Images, R Jens Stolt/Shutterstock.com. 12: M Helga Esteb/Shutterstock.com. 13: TL Debby Wong/Shutterstock.com, TR Joe Seer/Shutterstock.com, BL Helga Esteb/Shutterstock.com, BR TM&©20thC.Fox/Everett/Rex Features. 14: BG D_D/Africa Studio/Shutterstock.com, L Joe Seer/Shutterstock.com, R Helga Esteb/Shutterstock.com. 15: L Helga Esteb/Shutterstock.com. 16: BG Fesus Robert/Shutterstock.com, L Noel Vasquez/Getty Images, R Helga Esteb/Shutterstock.com. 17: L Kevin Mazur/WireImage, R Helga Esteb/Shutterstock.com. 18: BG vovan/Shutterstock.com, L Donna Ward/Getty Images, BR Kostenko Maxim/Shutterstock.com. 19: Left Eyed Photography/Shutterstock.com. 20: BG Piko72/Shutterstock.com, R Joe Seer/Shutterstock.com, BL Helga Esteb/Shutterstock.com. 21: TR Newspix/Rex Features, BL Angela Weiss/Getty Images for Oakley. 22: BG Oliver Herold/Wikimedia Commons, L Donna Ward/Getty Images. 23: TL Jason Merritt/Getty Images, BR Marcel Thomas/FilmMagic. 24: L Jason Merritt/Getty Images, BR Kostenko Maxim/Shutterstock.com. 25: TL Artur Synenko/Shutterstock.com, R Jeff Vespa/WireImage. 26: BG Evgeny Dubinchuk/Shutterstock.com, BL EtiAmmos/Shutterstock.com. 27: ML & MR Nejron Photo/Shutterstock.com. 28: BG andreiuc88/Shutterstock.com, BR Jeff Wilber/Shutterstock.com, BR Roman Sigaev/Shutterstock.com. 29: BL Ken McKay/ITV/Rex Features, R Canadian Press/Rex Features. 30: BG Serg64/Shutterstock.com, TL KdEdesign/Shutterstock.com, R Billy Farrell Agency/Rex Features. 31: R Most Wanted/Rex Features, BL Tom Grundy/Shutterstock.com. 32: BL Eric Charbonneau/WireImage, BR Peter Dazeley/Photographer's Choice. 33: R Jason Merritt/Getty Images. 34: BL Dfree/Shutterstock.com, BR gualtiero boffi/Shutterstock.com. 35: BL Kostenko Maxim/Shutterstock.com, R Chelsea Lauren/Getty Images. 36: BG Stefan Glebowski/Shutterstock.com, ML Thorsten Rust/Shutterstock.com, BR Frederick M. Brown/Getty Images. 37: BG twistah/Shutterstock.com, TL Michael Buckner/WireImage. 38: BG Carston Medom Madsen/Shutterstock.com, ML SVLuma/Shutterstock.com. 39: BG David Maska/Shutterstock.com. 40: BG stevanovic.igor/Shutterstock.com, BL Kris Connor/Getty Images, BR Michael Buckner/WireImage. 41: M Henry Lamb/Photowire/BEI/Rex Features, R Helga Esteb/Shutterstock.com. 42: BG Rui Vale de Sousa/Shutterstock.com, TL Marcel Thomas/FilmMagic, MR irin-k/Shutterstock.com, L Africa Studio/Shutterstock.com. 43: TL Konstantin Mironov/Shutterstock.com, TR Dmitry Naumov/Shutterstock.com, MR Canadian Press/Rex Features, BR cynoclub/Shutterstock.com. 44: BG fuyu liu & leungchopan/Shutterstock.com. 45: BG Semisatch/Shutterstock.com, TL marco mayer/Shutterstock.com, TR MikeE/Shutterstock.com, BL Robert Milek/Shutterstock.com, BR:Valentyn Volkov/Shutterstock.com. 46: BG leungchopan/Shutterstock.com, L:Joe Seer/Shutterstock.com. 47: TR Helga Esteb/Shutterstock.com, ML Richard Young/Rex Features, BR Joe Seer/Shutterstock.com. 48: BG Fesus Robert/Shutterstock.com, L Helga Esteb/Shutterstock.com. 49: L carrie-nelson/Shutterstock.com. 50: BG javarman/Shutterstock.com, LtoR, TtoB: as p24, as p47, as p49, as p43, Dfree/Shutterstock.com, as p40. 51: LtoR, TtoB: as p47, as p40, Noel Vasquez/Getty Images, as p33, as p32, as p10, as p23. 52: BG Fesus Robert/Shutterstock.com, L as p50. 53: BL Helga Esteb/Shutterstock.com, BR as p51. 54: BG Konstantin Sutyagin/Shutterstock.com, L as p18, BR Gunnar Pippel/Shutterstock.com. 55: T cinemafestival/Shutterstock.com, TR Rudchenko Liliia/Shutterstock.com, BL Francesco Scotto/Shutterstock.com, BR Debby Wong/Shutterstock.com. 56: L as p14, BR andreiuc88/Shutterstock.com. 57: BG Flashworks/iStock, TR Jens Stolt/Shutterstock.com, BR Rena Schild/Shutterstock.com. 58: BG Fesus Robert/Shutterstock.com, R Startraks Photo/Rex Features, M as p42, BL Mike Truchon/Shutterstock.com. 59: TL Startraks Photo/Rex Features, MR Evgeny Dubinchuk/Shutterstock.com, BL Jim Smeal/BEI/Rex Features. 60: BG Losevsky Pavel/Shutterstock.com. 61: BG Pereira da Mata/Shutterstock.com, BR Helga Esteb/Shutterstock.com. 62: BG as p2, BL as p2. 63: as p2. Text panels (used throughout): R-studio/ilolab/Brian Weed/Valentin Agapov/viki2win/javarman/silver-john/Valeev/Nomad_Soul/Vlue/szefei/photocell/Sinelyov/Volodymyr Krasyuk/karamysh/Shutterstock.com.

MIX
Paper from
responsible sources
FSC® C016897

The Random House Group Limited supports The Forest Stewardship Council (FSC®), the leading international forest certification organisation. Our books carrying the FSC label are printed on FSC® certified paper. FSC is the only forest certification scheme endorsed by the leading environmental organisations, including Greenpeace. Our paper procurement policy can be found at www.randomhouse.co.uk/environment

Bantam Books are published by Random House Children's Books, 61–63 Uxbridge Road, London W5 5SA

www.totallyrandombooks.co.uk
www.rbooks.co.uk

Addresses for companies within The Random House Group Limited can be found at: www.randomhouse.co.uk/offices.htm

THE RANDOM HOUSE GROUP Limited Reg. No. 954009

A CIP catalogue record for this book is available from the British Library.

Printed in Italy

100% UNOFFICIAL TRIBUTE TO THE HUNGER GAMES

PAGE 10
Katniss Everdeen

PAGE 24
Team Gale or Team Peeta?

PAGE 48
Effie Trinket

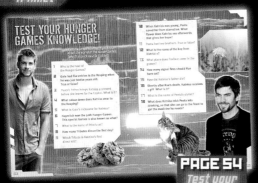

PAGE 54
Test your knowledge

CONTENTS

WELCOME TO THE 100% UNOFFICIAL TRIBUTE TO THE HUNGER GAMES!

The Hunger Games is so hot it's practically on fire! Based on an amazing trilogy of action-packed books, the movie is set to take the world by storm with its super-cute cast, wicked stunts and tantalising love triangle. It's not just about teen love either – there's a deeper message to *The Hunger Games*. Let us guide you through the world of the Games – but be warned, it is truly dark and dangerous . . .

You're about to enter Panem, a cruel place where only the strong survive. Panem consists of twelve Districts, which all work hard to make food, clothes and fuel for the wealthy Capitol that controls them. The Capitol likes to show the Districts exactly who's boss, so every year a boy and girl from each of the Districts must travel to the Arena to take part in the Hunger Games – a fight to the death in front of the TV cameras.

This year, going into the Games is 16-year old Katniss Everdeen from District 12, who can wield a mean bow and arrows and is determined to get home to her family and her best friend, Gale. Alongside her is Peeta Mellark, the boy who claims he's got a massive crush on her. There can only be one winner and just wait until you see Katniss in action . . .

The Hunger Games trilogy was written by the talented Suzanne Collins, and since the first book was published, die-hard fans have been counting the days until they can see Katniss brought to life on the big screen. And not only do we have the brilliant movie of *The Hunger Games* to enjoy, but there are two more books in the series, *Catching Fire* and *Mockingjay*, to look forward to. We can't wait!

DID YOU KNOW?

Suzanne Collins has talked about her original idea for The Hunger Games - it was inspired by some late night channel hopping: "One night, I was lying in bed, and I was channel surfing between reality TV programs and actual war coverage... I was really tired, and the lines between these stories started to blur in a very unsettling way. That's the moment when Katniss's story came to me."

"Katniss, the girl who was on fire."
Cinna

Gary Ross

With all its colourful characters, dramatic settings and amazing costumes, making *The Hunger Games* into a movie was no mean feat. But with a roll call of brilliant behind-the-scenes talent, amazing A-listers and hot young newbies, we're totally thrilled about the movie. Let us tell you why . . .

 Writer and ultimate HG guru Suzanne Collins has been completely involved in the process, discussing every last detail with director Gary Ross and even doing the first draft of the script.

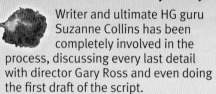

 As well as a fabulous script, there's a whole host of excellent actors, from super-fit stunt people to veteran Hollywood legends, with plenty of fresh new faces to watch out for. The cast all got on amazingly well on set, even though they spent most of the time trying to kill each other! They were also kept busy doing plenty of stunt and fight training, so those battle scenes would be just perfect.

 The movie was filmed in the beautiful US state of North Carolina, which has plenty of stunning forests to replicate the woody landscape of the Arena. It was reported that the city of Shelby stood in for District 12, with the set designers creating the Hob, train station and other important buildings. The sets were kept absolutely top secret to stop any spoilers leaking out, which just makes us even more eager to see what they've got up their sleeves for those fireballs, battles and tender moments.

We're also excited to hear the music that movie legends T-Bone Burnett and Danny Elfman have put together. T-Bone Burnett has worked on *O Brother, Where Art Thou*, *Crazy Heart* and *Walk the Line*, while Danny Elfman has worked on *Charlie and the Chocolate Factory*, *Desperate Housewives* and the *Spider-Man* films. That will be some totally amazing music! T-Bone has written a special lullaby for Katniss to sing to Rue, which is one of the most tear-jerking moments of the book, and T-Bone has talked about how beautiful Jennifer's voice is. We're getting goosebumps already . . .

T-Bone Burnett

Danny Elfman

CELEB FANS

It's not just us going crazy for The Hunger Games *– loads of celebs have been telling the world just how much they love Suzanne Collins' amazing trilogy!*

It was rumoured that *True Grit* star, and Jennifer Lawrence's fellow 2011 Oscar nominee, Hailee Steinfeld auditioned for the part of Katniss. What we know for sure is that she's a big fan of the books, and of Jennifer: "Jennifer looks insane in character as Katniss. Amazing, I am so excited. I'm a huge fan of the books. I love, love the cast. As a fan of the books, I think they have it right on."

Awesome actor Robert Pattinson, who played our favourite vampire in the *Twilight* movies, has also discovered *The Hunger Games*: "I sort of came across it last year, and I didn't realize it was the most enormous thing in the world. It's good! It will be a good movie." The films that made Robert a superstar and a heartthrob also came from a series of hit books, written by the talented Stephenie Meyer.

Robert Pattinson

The Devil Wears Prada actress Emily Blunt found the books both scary and spellbinding: "I'm kind of riveted by it and terrified by it at the same time. I can't stop reading it." The plot running through *The Hunger Games* trilogy is truly gripping, so we can totally understand why Emily wouldn't want to put the books down!

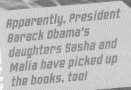
Emily Blunt

Emma Roberts, who is the niece of famous actress Julia Roberts and is also an up-and-coming actress herself, has been telling all her friends about *The Hunger Games*, just like we have: "I'm really excited to see the movie. I read all the books a couple weeks ago, and I've got all my friends hooked. It's totally cool and I can't wait to see it." Time for a girls' night out to the cinema then!

DID YOU KNOW? Apparently, President Barack Obama's daughters Sasha and Malia have picked up the books, too!

Emma Roberts

KATNISS EVERDEEN

She's the star of the Hunger Games, so let's see why...

Smart, strong and savvy, Katniss Everdeen has been a survivor right from the start. Her father died in a mine explosion when she was 11, leaving her mother with severe depression and unable to care for her children. Seeing her gentle-natured little sister, Prim, wasting away was heartbreaking, so a weak and frail Katniss searched for food in the bins of the wealthier families in District 12.

Peeta's mother caught Katniss and turned her away, but Peeta was kinder. He deliberately burnt two loaves of bread, knowing he would be punished, and gave them to her. This allowed Katniss to feed her family, and gave her strength and hope.

Katniss took to the woods to hunt. Her father had taught her how to use a bow and arrows and with practice she became an expert. It was here that she met her best friend Gale, who taught her how to make snares, and together they sold food illegally at the Hob. Gale made Katniss smile again.

When Prim is picked at the Reaping, Katniss is horrified and quickly volunteers to take her place. She loves her little sister more than anything in the world and would give her life to protect her. And whilst she is conflicted when Peeta's name is also picked, because she still feels like she owes 'the boy with the bread' for saving her life, Katniss promised Prim that she would try to win the Games. Her struggle to survive all her life has prepared Katniss well for the Arena and she is determined to return home to her family. Our money is definitely on Katniss, to win!

Willow Shields plays Prim Everdeen

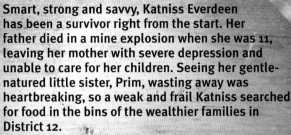

Paula Malcomson plays Mrs Everdeen

"The cool thing about Katniss is that every fan has such a personal relationship with her. I'm a massive fan too, so I get it. She's incredibly powerful, brave, and tough - and yet she has a tenderness and complexity."

Jennifer Lawrence

"I've done archery…
and rock climbing,
tree climbing – and
combat, running and
vaulting. But also
yoga and things like
that, to stay catlike!"
Jennifer Lawrence

JENNIFER LAWRENCE

Let's take a closer look at the lovely leading lady . . .

"Jen is perfectly cast. She's amazing. The real deal. Honestly, when we shot the Reaping, I wept."
Elizabeth Banks

"Jennifer Lawrence... has so much depth and power and talent and sophistication and sensitivity and subtlety that she's become Katniss Everdeen synonymously."
Gary Ross, Director

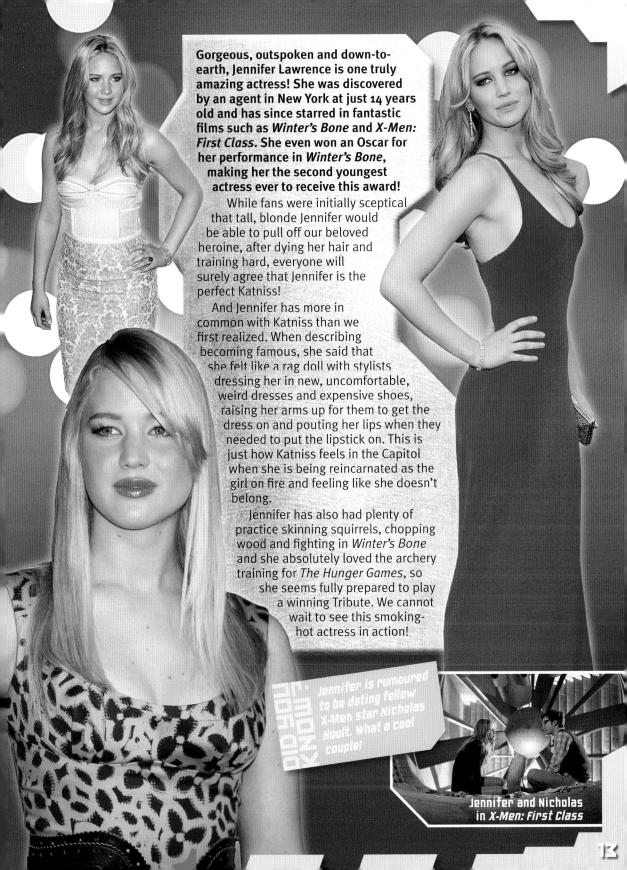

Gorgeous, outspoken and down-to-earth, Jennifer Lawrence is one truly amazing actress! She was discovered by an agent in New York at just 14 years old and has since starred in fantastic films such as *Winter's Bone* and *X-Men: First Class*. She even won an Oscar for her performance in *Winter's Bone*, making her the second youngest actress ever to receive this award!

While fans were initially sceptical that tall, blonde Jennifer would be able to pull off our beloved heroine, after dying her hair and training hard, everyone will surely agree that Jennifer is the perfect Katniss!

And Jennifer has more in common with Katniss than we first realized. When describing becoming famous, she said that she felt like a rag doll with stylists dressing her in new, uncomfortable, weird dresses and expensive shoes, raising her arms up for them to get the dress on and pouting her lips when they needed to put the lipstick on. This is just how Katniss feels in the Capitol when she is being reincarnated as the girl on fire and feeling like she doesn't belong.

Jennifer has also had plenty of practice skinning squirrels, chopping wood and fighting in *Winter's Bone* and she absolutely loved the archery training for *The Hunger Games*, so she seems fully prepared to play a winning Tribute. We cannot wait to see this smoking-hot actress in action!

DID YOU KNOW?

Jennifer is rumoured to be dating fellow X-Men star Nicholas Hoult. What a cool couple!

Jennifer and Nicholas in *X-Men: First Class*

13

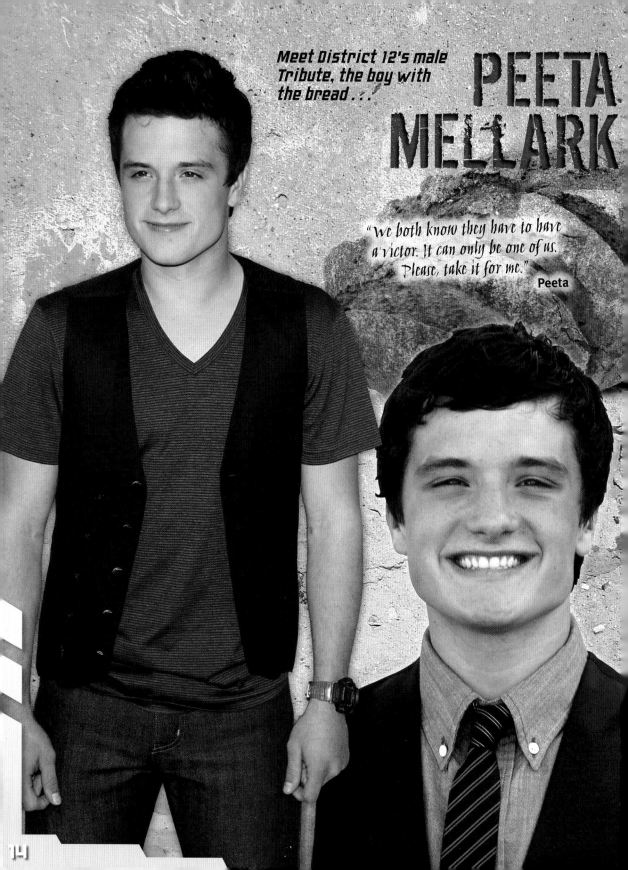

Meet District 12's male Tribute, the boy with the bread . . .

PEETA MELLARK

"We both know they have to have a victor. It can only be one of us. Please, take it for me."

Peeta

> *"Remember we're madly in love, so it's all right to kiss me any time you feel like it."*
>
> Peeta

Peeta Malark has a super-stocky build, with ashy blond hair and beautiful blue eyes. He's also kind-natured, charming and instantly likeable, so it's easy to see why Katniss would begin to fall for him! Peeta is a bakers son, which makes him wealthier than most families in District 12, but his childhood was still tough. Although his father is kind and generous, his mother seems cold and harsh – on Reaping day she even tells Peeta that she doesn't expect him to return home!

And Peeta has an even tougher time when Katniss, the girl he's secretly had a crush on since he was 5 years old and never had the courage to speak to, is also picked for the Games as one of his competitors. Peeta is determined to help Katniss win.

When they finally team up near the end of the Hunger Games, Peeta makes it clear to Katniss that his publicised love for her was no lie. Katniss knows she must continue to pretend to love Peeta in return because the cameras are watching, but she does begin to secretly develop romantic feelings for him, too.

However, when they both win the Games, Katniss begins to have doubts. She knows she must tell Peeta that she has mostly been acting and when Peeta finds out, he is devastated. Broken-hearted, Peeta tells Katniss to let him know when she figures out what she really wants and we are left wondering what will become of the star-crossed lovers from District 12 . . .

JOSH HUTCHERSON

Find out why he's perfect to play the part of Peeta...

Josh and Vanessa at a basketball match, March 2011

"I am Peeta. His humility, his self-deprecating humour, his way that he can just talk to anybody in the room."

Josh Hutcherson

"If Josh had been bright purple and had wings and gave that audition, I'd have been like 'Cast him! We can work around the wings!' He was that good."

Suzanne Collins

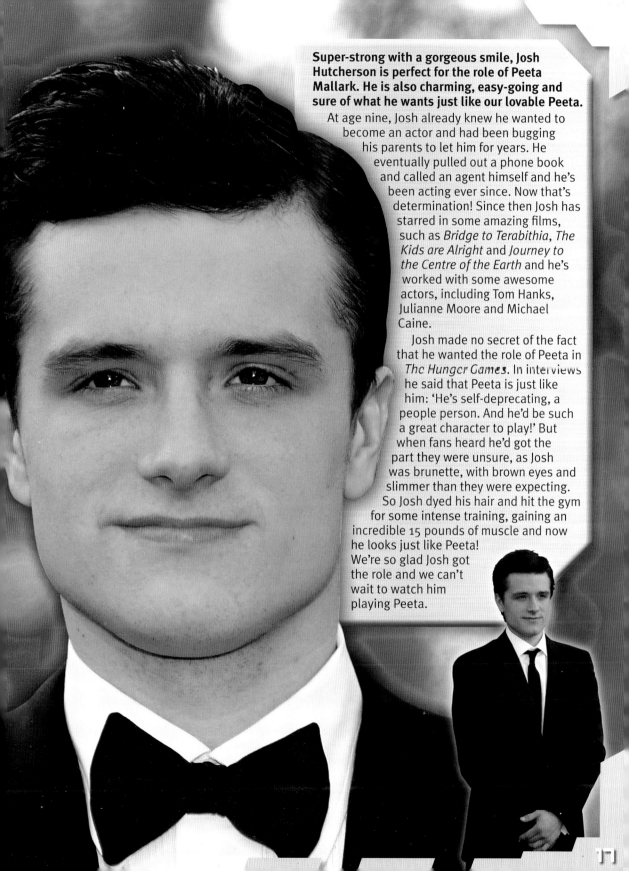

Super-strong with a gorgeous smile, Josh Hutcherson is perfect for the role of Peeta Mallark. He is also charming, easy-going and sure of what he wants just like our lovable Peeta.

At age nine, Josh already knew he wanted to become an actor and had been bugging his parents to let him for years. He eventually pulled out a phone book and called an agent himself and he's been acting ever since. Now that's determination! Since then Josh has starred in some amazing films, such as *Bridge to Terabithia*, *The Kids are Alright* and *Journey to the Centre of the Earth* and he's worked with some awesome actors, including Tom Hanks, Julianne Moore and Michael Caine.

Josh made no secret of the fact that he wanted the role of Peeta in *The Hunger Games*. In interviews he said that Peeta is just like him: 'He's self-deprecating, a people person. And he'd be such a great character to play!' But when fans heard he'd got the part they were unsure, as Josh was brunette, with brown eyes and slimmer than they were expecting. So Josh dyed his hair and hit the gym for some intense training, gaining an incredible 15 pounds of muscle and now he looks just like Peeta! We're so glad Josh got the role and we can't wait to watch him playing Peeta.

GALE HAWTHORNE

Discover why he's Katniss's best buddy and her perfect hunting partner . . .

Gale is Katniss' best friend, hunting partner and perhaps something more . . . And as he's six feet tall, lean and hard-muscled, with gorgeous grey eyes and olive skin, who would blame her?

Gale is strong, kind and caring, too. His father died in the same mining explosion as Katniss' father, leaving him to take care of his mother, two younger brothers and his younger sister. He immediately began hunting for food for his family in the woods and, at age 14, he met Katniss and formed a strong hunting partnership with her.

Like Katniss, he can be stubborn and has a temper – he resents the fact that they must struggle to survive and often rants to Katniss, in private, about the Capitol's oppressive control over the 12 Districts of Panem and how cruel and inhumane the Hunger Games are.

We can tell Gale cares deeply for Katniss when, just before the Reaping, he suggests they run away together to escape selection for the Games and when Katniss volunteers to take Prim's place he struggles to keep his emotions under control. In the Justice Building, he tells Katniss that he knows she can win and promises to protect and help her family in her absence.

In the Arena, his voice is constantly in Katniss's head and when she begins to develop feelings for Peeta, she feels guilty because she is confused about her relationship with Gale. She worries what he will think and say when they return home to District 12 . . .

"As everyone knows, Gale is an enormous part of Katniss' life... he's in her head, he's in her life, he's something that echoes with her throughout the games."
Gary Ross, Director

LIAM HEMSWORTH

Here's more about the gorgeous guy who will be Gale . . .

Liam wanted the role of Gale so badly that he said he would burn down his own house if the role went to someone else! With that passion, it sounds like Liam is perfect for the role of Gale!

Liam and his brother Chris at the premiere of *Thor*

With a buff body and boyish good looks it's no wonder luscious Liam ended up in front of the cameras!

Born in Australia, Liam began acting in popular Aussie soaps like *Neighbours* and *Home and Away*, before moving to LA to pursue his dream. He had reportedly only been living in LA for a few weeks, and hadn't even found an agent yet, when he was snapped up to star as Miley Cyrus's love interest in *The Last Song*. Miley soon became Liam's girlfriend in real life – now that's one lucky leading lady!

His brothers, Luke and Chris Hemsworth are also famous actors and they were his inspiration for choosing a career in acting. In fact, both Liam and Chris were considered for the lead role in *Thor*.

The part eventually went to Chris but there is definitely no bad blood between these brothers – when Liam prepared for the role of Gale in *The Hunger Games*, Chris read lines with him for hours, even putting on the girly voice of Katniss in the hope that it would help Liam secure the role. That's brotherly love!

When he's not learning lines, Liam loves surfing and playing Australian football. It's no wonder he's so fit!

Liam and Miley, Sydney, June 2011

Liam snowboarding in Utah, Jan 2011

DID YOU KNOW?

While Gale and Peeta will surely dislike one another in The Hunger Games, Liam and Josh bonded so well during their weeks on set together that Josh took Liam to his home in Kentucky one weekend to chill with his family. There's even rumours that they might share an apartment together. We'd love to be a fly on the wall in their new pad!

"Liam is just a solid brick of muscle but he's got depth and he's interesting and at the same time he's natural and he flows."
Jennifer Lawrence

THE BEGINNING OF THE LOVE TRIANGLE

Katniss Everdeen has never given much thought to love and romance but lately, she's had to think about it, whether she likes it or not . . .

"I push the whole thing out of my mind, because for some reason Gale and Peeta do not coexist well together in my thoughts."
Katniss

KATNISS

Katniss sees all the attention her friend Gale gets from the other girls and she can understand it; he's good-looking, strong, can hunt. She admits that it does make her jealous, but not for *those* reasons – she just doesn't want to lose her hunting partner. She also knows that the word "friend" isn't quite right for someone who helps her to keep her family alive and who's so familiar to her.

And then there's Peeta Mellark. Katniss can't believe that of all people, she has to go into the Arena with Peeta! He's a reminder of a very dark time, but also of hope. When Katniss and her family were at their very worst, she stole scraps of food from people's rubbish and was thrown some burnt bread by Peeta. She later realised that he burnt the bread deliberately and was hit by his mother for doing so. She feels uncomfortable about owing him this debt.

That's when things start to get confusing. Peeta tells the entire world he has a crush on her, turning them into star-crossed lovers! Now Katniss has to pretend that she has feelings for him, too, whilst thinking of Gale watching them back home. But is she really just pretending? Either way, Katniss knows she'll have to make up her mind before too long . . .

"I feel Gale's grey eyes watching me watching Peeta, all the way from District 12."
Katniss

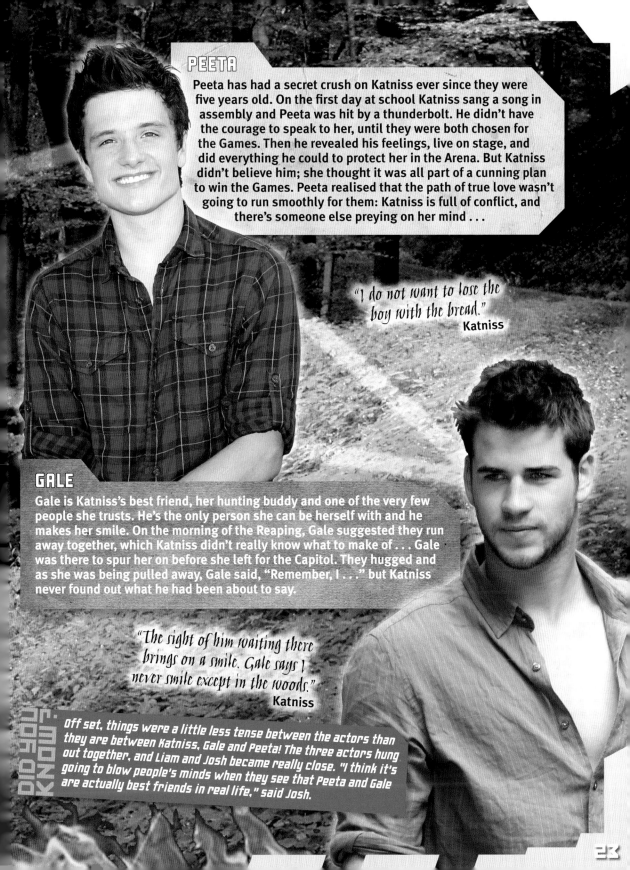

PEETA

Peeta has had a secret crush on Katniss ever since they were five years old. On the first day at school Katniss sang a song in assembly and Peeta was hit by a thunderbolt. He didn't have the courage to speak to her, until they were both chosen for the Games. Then he revealed his feelings, live on stage, and did everything he could to protect her in the Arena. But Katniss didn't believe him; she thought it was all part of a cunning plan to win the Games. Peeta realised that the path of true love wasn't going to run smoothly for them: Katniss is full of conflict, and there's someone else preying on her mind . . .

"I do not want to lose the boy with the bread."
Katniss

GALE

Gale is Katniss's best friend, her hunting buddy and one of the very few people she trusts. He's the only person she can be herself with and he makes her smile. On the morning of the Reaping, Gale suggested they run away together, which Katniss didn't really know what to make of . . . Gale was there to spur her on before she left for the Capitol. They hugged and as she was being pulled away, Gale said, "Remember, I . . ." but Katniss never found out what he had been about to say.

"The sight of him waiting there brings on a smile. Gale says I never smile except in the woods."
Katniss

DID YOU KNOW?
Off set, things were a little less tense between the actors than they are between Katniss, Gale and Peeta! The three actors hung out together, and Liam and Josh became really close. "I think it's going to blow people's minds when they see that Peeta and Gale are actually best friends in real life," said Josh.

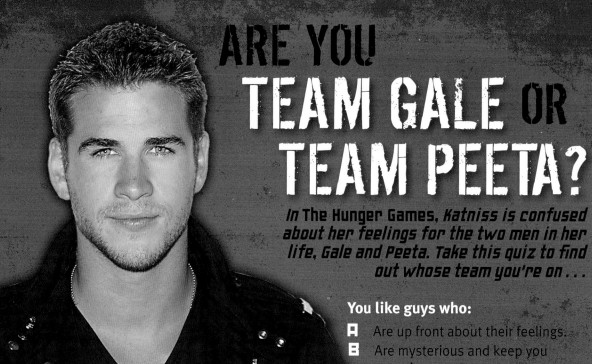

ARE YOU TEAM GALE OR TEAM PEETA?

In **The Hunger Games**, Katniss is confused about her feelings for the two men in her life, Gale and Peeta. Take this quiz to find out whose team you're on . . .

You like guys who:

A Are up front about their feelings.

B Are mysterious and keep you guessing.

You love a guy with:

A Golden hair and blue eyes.

B Dark hair and olive skin.

You like guys who are:

A Sensitive and thoughtful.

B Brave and fearless.

On a perfect day with your guy, you would:

A Stay inside, talk and kiss.

B Head outside to run around the woods together.

You like guys who smell like:

A Bread.

B Woodsmoke.

GALE

Your ideal guy is:

A Artistic.
B Practical.

You like it if your guy:

A Is shy around girls.
B Has lots of other girls interested in him.

Your dream guy is:

A The youngest in his family.
B The oldest in his family.

You like a guy who is:

A Broad-shouldered and quick.
B Stocky and strong.

Your perfect guy is:

A The strong, silent type.
B A charmer who tells good jokes.

Mostly As: You're Team Peeta! You like a sensitive guy who's completely devoted to you.

Mostly Bs: You're Team Gale! You like a man of mystery who loves to have an adventure.

ABOUT THE GAMES

Let's get the low-down on the most anticipated event of the year . . .

THE WORLD OF THE HUNGER GAMES

Over the years, North America was hit by many disasters, until all that was left of it was the country of Panem. Panem was split into thirteen Districts, each focusing on creating one product for the Capitol. But then came the Dark Days, when the Districts rebelled against the Capitol. Twelve Districts were overpowered, and District 13 was destroyed. The Capitol decided on new, stricter ways to keep the Districts in line in the future. Things got worse for people in many of the Districts, as they worked their fingers to the bone making produce for the Capitol, without having enough themselves. Most people are very poor – they don't have much food and they live under strict rules. The Capitol reminds the Districts how powerful they are by showing the smoking ruins of District 13 on TV and with the annual Hunger Games.

THE GAMES: THE REAPING

To remind the people that they must never rebel again, every year there is a Reaping in each District. Residents are eligible to be in the Reaping between the ages of twelve and eighteen. One boy's name and one girl's name are picked out at random. These boys and girls make up the twenty-four Tributes that are sent into the Arena to fight to the death.

Normally, your name only goes into the Reaping once, but if you are poor, you can sign up for tesserae – a years' supply of grain and oil – and your name goes in more times. Katniss signs up for three tesserae, for her and her mother and Prim, which means her name goes into the hat four times all together. This builds up over the years too, so Katniss's name is in the pot twenty times when she is sixteen, while twelve year old Prim's name is only in once.

For the 74th Hunger Games, the Tributes picked out for District 12 are Primrose Everdeen and Peeta Mellark. But Katniss Everdeen volunteers to take her little sister's place . . .

DID YOU KNOW? After the Games, the Arenas become tourist destinations, where people from the Capitol can visit and take part in re-enactments.

"With one sweep of my arm, I push her behind me. 'I volunteer!' I gasp. 'I volunteer as Tribute!'"
Katniss

THE GAMES: PREPARATION

After the Reaping, Tributes must travel to the Capitol to train. They learn survival skills, like using weapons, camouflage, making fires and identifying wild plants.

The Tributes are given a rating by the Gamemakers, based on their level of skills – a high mark will help get sponsors, and sponsors will send special gifts in the Arena.

The Tributes are each given their own team of stylists. They will take part in an elaborate procession and have TV interviews in the Capitol and it's important to make a good impression here – clothes, hair and make-up can all help.

THE GAMES: THE ARENA

The Games take place in the Arena, which changes every year. It can be cold or hot, wet or dry, hilly or flat.

The only rule is that Tributes must stand on their metal launch pads for sixty seconds, before being set free into the Games. The launch pads are all positioned around the Cornucopia, which is filled with food, weapons and other useful survival items at the beginning of the Games. However, if you want to get these items, you'll be running into a vicious battle . . .

THE GAMES: BACK IN PANEM

Once the Games begin, everyone must watch them, often on big screens in the Districts. The Games are hugely entertaining for the people of the Capitol, where everyone gossips about their favourite Tributes and places bets on who will win.

The Gamemakers control the Arena. If nothing interesting is happening, they can change the environment, for instance with fires or floods that will force Tributes together for battles.

The mentors for each District seek sponsors for their Tributes, who will give money for gifts. This can be hugely important for the Tributes, so it's essential to give potential sponsors a good show.

THE GAMES: THE WINNER

There can only be one winner. The prize is gifts for them and their District, including a new house for the Tribute's family to live in, plenty of food and luxuries, like sugar, grain and oil. The winner must also tour Panem after the Games have finished.

Katniss doesn't think she has any chance of winning the Hunger Games. Though it isn't really allowed, in the richer Districts like Districts 1, 2 and 4, children train all year for the Games. They think that taking part is a big honour. These are the Career Tributes: often brutal and strong, and happy to gang up together at first against the other Tributes.

THE MENTOR: HAYMITCH ABERNATHY

It's time to meet Katniss and Peeta's mentor . . .

HAYMITCH ABERNATHY

Sarcastic, surly and often drunk and disorderly, Haymitch Abernathy is one of only two Tributes from District 12 ever to have won the Hunger Games. He has been made to mentor Tributes from his deprived District every year since. When Katniss volunteers for Prim at the Reaping, Haymitch staggers to the stage, impressed that she has shown some 'spunk', only to then fall off into the crowd. He is even more impressed later, in the Capitol, when Peeta lashes out at him and Katniss throws a knife to block him from his alcohol supply. Haymitch finally realizes that they might have a chance of winning the Games after all, and so from then on, he is hard and harsh, training them to fight and win.

Haymitch is also super-smart and although he is absent from the Arena, he creates a brilliant form of communication with Katniss through her food supply. She is able to work out that Haymitch would only deprive her of water if she was extremely close to finding it herself, so she soldiers on and finally reaches a pond. When she displays her 'love' for Peeta, more supplies arrive; Haymitch rewards her when she does something he and the people of the Capitol approve of. This forges a strong bond between Haymitch and Katniss and when she leaves the Arena, he is the first person she hugs and thanks. So, whilst Haymitch pretends to be hard and unfeeling, it's obvious by the end that he actually cares a great deal for both Peeta and Katniss.

> "Well what's this? . . . Did I actually get a pair of fighters this year?"
> **Haymitch**

> "Haymitch couldn't be sending me a clearer message. One kiss equals one pot of broth. I can almost hear his snarl. You're supposed to be in love, sweetheart. The boy's dying. Give me something I can work with!"
> **Katniss**

WOODY HARRELSON

We think Woody Harrelson is the perfect person to play Katniss and Peeta's mentor, Haymitch. We already know he can act a comical drunk from his role in comedy film, *Kingpin*. He's also starred in amazing films such as *No Country for Old Men*, *The Messenger* and *Zombieland* but is probably best known for his TV role in *Cheers*. Like Haymitch, Harrelson is used to being a victor. When he came to the UK and took part in Soccer Aid at Old Trafford, to raise money for UNICEF, he played for the 'Rest of the World' team and came on for the last 15 minutes to score the winning goal in the penalty shootout. We can't wait to see Harrelson bring super-sarcastic victor Haymitch to life!

Woody at Old Trafford

"Haymitch is such an unforgettable character: funny cranky outrageous, sarcastic, impatient, biting but ultimately kind. I'm so grateful we have Woody Harrelson to play him."
Gary Ross, Director

DISTRICT 1

Wealthy and privileged, District 1 is close to the Capitol. It makes luxury items for the Capitol, such as diamonds. Children from District 1 are trained for the Games, so they are often brutal, strong and skilled with weapons. These Career Tributes are always favourites to win the Games and are feared by Tributes from other, poorer Districts.

FEMALE TRIBUTE

As her name suggests, Glimmer is gorgeous and glamorous. She knows how to use her good looks to make an impact and wears a see-through gold gown to her interview. However, as a Career Tribute she also has amazing skills in the Arena, and teams up with the Career pack. Glimmer infuriates Katniss by taking the bow and arrows left at the Cornucopia even though she has no skill with them.

TRIBUTE STATS:

NAME / NICKNAME: Glimmer

AGE: Unknown

DESCRIPTION: Tall, blonde hair and green eyes

TRAINING SCORE: Between 8 and 10

WEAPON OF CHOICE: She uses a bow and arrows in the Games, but isn't as good with it as Katniss, so her true skill probably lies with another weapon.

"She tries to shoot me and it's immediately evident that she's incompetent with a bow."
Katniss

PLAYED BY: Leven Rambin was born on 17th May, 1990. She has acted in the action-packed *Terminator: The Sarah Connor Chronicles*, as well as *Grey's Anatomy*, *CSI: Miami* and *One Tree Hill*. She also had not one but two parts on US soap *All My Children*, playing half-sisters. Her own sister is a handbag designer, which sounds right up glamourous Glimmer's avenue! Massive *Hunger Games* fan Leven trained hard to become ruthless Glimmer, doing tons of fight training, learning how to use swords and pushing herself to the limit to become the perfect Career Tribute.

Tribute Quote:

"I am such a big fan... Once I picked it up, I couldn't stop. I was constantly reading it: on airplanes, at dinner, I was reading it under the table." – Leven Rambin

> *"The boy from District 1 ignites a tree branch for a torch, illuminating the grim determination on their faces."*
> **Katniss**

MALE TRIBUTE:

Marvel is a Career Tribute. As well as having honed fighting skills, he knows how to work the crowd. He and Glimmer arrive on their chariot for the procession spray painted silver and wearing glittering jewel-covered tunics – what a look! He is a key part of the Career pack.

TRIBUTE STATS:

NAME / NICKNAME: Marvel
AGE: Unknown
DESCRIPTION: Unknown
TRAINING SCORE: Between 8 and 10
WEAPON OF CHOICE: Marvel is super-talented with a spear

PLAYED BY:

Jack Quaid was born 24th April, 1992. Though this is his first acting role, he has acting in his genes, having famous film actors as his parents. His mum is Meg Ryan, who starred in *When Harry Met Sally* and *Sleepless in Seattle* and his dad is Dennis Quaid from *The Day After Tomorrow* and *The Parent Trap*. Jack is also part of a comedy band, doing sketch comedy with his friends, and he is majoring in Acting at New York University. We can't wait to see what he does next!

DID YOU KNOW?
Jack put on over 7kgs of muscle before they started shooting the film and kept on working out during filming.

DID YOU KNOW?
In the book, the Gamemakers have to confiscate a ring with a poisoned spike that Glimmer wanted to wear into the Arena. She claims she didn't know that it was booby-trapped and that it was just a lucky charm, but we know Glimmer is ruthless and calculating enough to try that trick!

Tribute Tweet:

@JackQuaid92 "I'm going to miss everybody so much. I'm so thankful to be part of this wonderful cast and crew and I'm so lucky to call them my friends."

Publicly, District two is presented as the nation's stone quarries, but secretly it's where most of the Peacekeepers are trained and where the Capitol's deadliest weapons are manufactured. District 2's children are raised like warriors. Trained for the Games from a young age, these Career Tributes are often proud to be picked at the Reaping – they are always strong, surly and firm favourites to win.

FEMALE TRIBUTE:

Callous and cunning, Clove is the first Tribute to make her mark at the Cornucopia. She is a Career Tribute and is confident she can win the Games, no problem. She is a key member of the Career pack and she never shies away from confrontation. With her quick wits and even quicker reflexes, Clove is a real contender – she knows it and makes sure the other Tributes do, too.

TRIBUTE STATS:

NAME/NICKNAME: Clove
AGE: Unknown
DESCRIPTION: Dark hair and green eyes.
TRAINING SCORE: Between 8 and 10
WEAPON OF CHOICE: Clove is nifty with a knife.

"Yes, the girl from District 2, ten metres away running towards me..."
Katni

PLAYED BY: Isabelle Fuhrman was born 25th February 1997. She has had plenty of practice playing a cruel character – she starred in the psychological thriller *Orphan* as Esther, a disturbed orphan girl who manipulates her new family and then tries to kill them. When producer Leonardo Dicaprio saw her audition video, apparently he was so amazed at how well she played the creepy little girl that he said he wouldn't make the film without her. We think Isabelle is perfect for the role of Clove and can't wait to see her in action!

Tribute Tweets:

@isabellefuhrman "It is nice to know I'm adorable even when killing people in a movie :)"

Isabelle loved her hamster, Lola, so much that she took it to the Sundance Film Festival in 2007 for the premiere of her film, Hounddog. Isabelle sounds a lot more caring than her cold-hearted character!

MALE TRIBUTE:

Dangerous and deadly, with a terrible temper, Cato is another of the Career Tributes. He is determined to win and won't let anything, or anyone, stand in his way. He's a big, bossy boy and quickly takes the lead role in the Career pack, issuing instructions and delivering directions. Cato is a top Tribute and he will take some beating in the Arena – the other Tributes should beware.

"I believe Cato could easily lose his judgement in a fit of temper."
Katniss

TRIBUTE STATS:

NAME/NICKNAME: Cato

AGE: Unknown

DESCRIPTION: Extremely strong, monstrous.

TRAINING SCORE: 10

WEAPON OF CHOICE: Cato is seriously skillful with a sword.

PLAYED BY: **Alexander Ludwig** was born 7th May 1992. He began acting at age ten in a Harry Potter toy commercial and later went on to star in *The Seeker: The Dark is Rising* and most recently, Disney's *Race to Witch Mountain*. He is currently studying film, theatre and entrepreneurship at the University of Southern California. In his spare time, Alex loves competing in extreme freestyle ski competitions or surfing on the Californian coast. He's an avid athlete who water skies, plays tennis, basketball and ice hockey. We're sure those sporting skills will come in handy in *The Hunger Games* and, thankfully, Alexander seems lovely in real life!

DID YOU KNOW? Alexander is a gifted musician who is supposedly in discussions regarding a future recording contract. Watch this space!

DID YOU KNOW? Gorgeous Alexander is also a featured model in the 2011 Abercrombie campaign – we can't wait to see those pics!

Tribute Tweets:

@alexanderludwig "playing the bad guy is pretty fun..."

WHICH FEMALE TRIBUTE ARE YOU?

In a battle between two of the top Tributes, would you be most like Katniss or Clove? Answers these quick questions to find out...

The area you live in is:

A Shoddy and nothing to brag about.

B Better than most areas in your country.

If a swarm of wasps was coming towards you, would you:

A Stay hidden, then run in the opposite direction?

B Run until you find a lake or river to jump into?

Do you:

A Keep yourself to yourself. One amazing best friend is plenty.

B Have a big crowd of friends, but there's no one that you're really close to.

KATNISS

If one of your allies were in trouble, would you:

A Take some time to help?

B Move on – this is the Hunger Games, it's no place to get soppy?

What are your best qualities?

A You have no idea the effect you can have.

B You are fearless and determined.

What do you think of the Hunger Games?

A They are cruel, unfair and inhumane.

B It would be an honour to take part.

Could you survive alone?

A I can take care of myself pretty well.

B No, I'd need help to find food and supplies.

Are you:

A Warm as fire?

B Cold like stone?

Mostly As: You're caring and clever, like Katniss.

Mostly Bs: You're cool and competitive, like Clove.

DISTRICTS 3 AND 4

District 3 produces Panem's electronics, televisions and explosives. District 4's industry is fishing, which is often useful in the Games. Tributes from District 4 are Careers – they are strong swimmers and trident throwers.

DISTRICT 3 TRIBUTES:

The female Tribute is only in the Games for one day. Her image is the first to be projected into the sky, to be seen by the whole of Panem.

The Career pack recruits the scrawny, ashen-skinned male Tribute. He uses the landmines that surround the plates at the Cornucopia as booby traps to protect the Careers' food and supplies, but when Katniss blows it up, Cato is furious.

Tribute Tweet:
@IanNelson95 "Great books!!! ... So honored to be a part of it!"

PLAYED BY: **Kalia Prescott** had a small role in *Where The Wild Things Are*, and is a seriously talented stunt girl who has performed in *Spider Man 2*, *Santa Clause 3: The Escape Clause* and *Red Dawn*. Kalia has a black belt in Tae Kwon Do, so she's perfectly prepared for her action-packed scenes in *The Hunger Games*!

Ian Nelson's first role was in the 2011 historical drama, *Alone Yet Not Alone*. He has also attended Stagedoor Manor Summer Camp, where he won an award for Outstanding Achievement by a Leading Actor.

Kalia is a published author. Her short story made it into an anthology of young, gifted US writers.

Ian has been in the Macy's Thanksgiving Day Parade in New York for two years running!

DISTRICT 4 TRIBUTES:

The female Tribute teams up with the other Careers. She receives too many stings when Katniss drops the tracker jacker nest.

Surprisingly for a Career, the male Tribute is only in the Games for one day. He leaves the female Tribute to carry his District's hopes.

PLAYED BY: Gorgeous **Tara Macken** is half Filipina and half Irish, and was born in a car in Kuwait. She lived in the Middle East and then moved to Brunei, Borneo. She excels at rock climbing, gymnastics and dance, and loves to travel. She is the perfect choice to play a Career Tribute, as she's also a death-defying stunt woman!

Young **Ethan Jamieson** is a newcomer to the world of acting, having had a bit part in *One Tree Hill*. Like his District 4 character, Ethan loves to fish!

"The girl from District 4 staggers out of sight, although I wouldn't bet on her making it to the lake."

Katniss

Tribute Tweet:
@taramacken "Thank you north Carolina!!! It has been wonderful, on my way to la!"

Tara has also appeared in the LXD, the Legion of Extraordinary Dancers, alongside Jeremy Marinas, the male Tribute from District 10.

> *"Foxface! Leave it to her to come up with such a clever and risky idea!"*
> **Katniss**

DISTRICT 5 TRIBUTES:

Clever and crafty with sleek red hair and amber eyes, Foxface is definitely one of our favourite Tributes! She has a sneaky strategy to win: work alone, keep away from the carnage and quietly steal her competitors' food. She outsmarts the Careers by managing to manoeuvre past their lethal landmines, and rather than fighting at the feast, she simply sprints out, secures her backpack and quickly evacuates the area. When she steals some berries from Peeta and Katniss' food supply, she doesn't realise that they are actually poisonous Nightlock berries.

Very little is known about the male Tribute, as he is only in the Games for one day.

Tribute Tweet:

@jackie_emerson "Best summer of my life. Ive learned and grown so much. I will always remember this experience and the friends I made. I love you all! <3"

PLAYED BY: **Jacqueline Emerson** was born on 21st August 1994. Unlike her character, who is one of the most televised Tributes in the Games, Jackie is new to the acting world. Her audition must have been truly amazing for her to secure this awesome role!

Chris Mark was born with a heart condition and at age nine, he had to have an open heart bypass. Afterwards, Chris was able to exercise freely again and pursue his dream career. He is now a master at Martial Arts, a spectacular stuntman and is great at gymnastics. He's performed stunts in amazing action films such as *Jumper*, *The Mummy 3* and *Kick Ass*!

DID YOU KNOW? Chris was Michael Cera's stunt double in Scott Pilgrim vs. the World, which we think is pretty impressive!

DISTRICT 6 TRIBUTES:

Both the female and male Tributes from District 6 are only in the Games for one day.

DID YOU KNOW? Kara is a member of DBX Stunts and she specializes in Russian swing, high falls and bungees!

PLAYED BY: **Kara Petersen** is a professional gymnast and stuntwoman. She's performed stunts in TV shows *Wizards of Waverly Place*, *A.N.T. Farm* and *Make It or Break It* and she's recently acted as a stunt double in awesome movie, *Super 8*!

Aston Moio has a black belt in Tae Kwon Do and has performed stunts in fantastic films like *Let Me In*, *The Longest Yard* and *Hop*. We bet he'll be at the heart of the Cornucopia carnage!

DID YOU KNOW? Aston also had a small supporting role in the TV show Dexter.

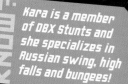

Tribute Tweet:

@KaraGPetersen "Thanks @taramacken for a good day of training!"

DISTRICTS 7 AND 8

District 7 produces lumber, so their Tributes often use axes as weapons. They have had a previous winner in the Games, Johanna Mason. She won through wily means - she pretended to be pathetic until only a few Tributes were left, and then she turned on them.

The citizens of District 8 produce textiles, including the uniforms that the Peacekeepers wear.

DISTRICT 7 TRIBUTES:

Both Tributes from District 7 are only in the Games for one day.

PLAYED BY: **Leigha Hancock** is an amazing gymnast and super-talented stunt performer, so we can't wait to see what she comes up with in the Games!

Sam Ly was born 21st September, 1988 in California. He has had minor roles in films like *Tremors 4: The Legend Begins* and *Timecop: The Berlin Decision*, but being cast in *The Hunger Games* is definitely his biggest break so far!

> **DID YOU KNOW?** Like Leigha and so many of the actors playing Tributes, Sam is an excellent stunt performer, which should come in handy in the Arena!

"The fire starter must have dozed off. They're on her before she can escape."

Katniss

Tribute Tweet:

@LeighaKayleen "Cast goodbye bon fire, packing & then heading to the airport at 5:30am...ouchhhh this hurts worse than the cornucopia ;)"

DISTRICT 8 TRIBUTES:

On the first night of the Hunger Games, Katniss has safely hidden up a tree, when along comes the female Tribute from District 8. She lights a fire, which leads the Career pack straight to her.

The male Tribute from District 8 is only in the Games for one day.

> **DID YOU KNOW?** Super-cute Samuel has also appeared in adverts for both Levis and Ray Bans.

PLAYED BY: **Mackenzie Lintz** is from a totally talented acting family. Her mum has been acting for over 15 years, and has appeared in *One Tree Hill*. Mackenzie's two brothers and sister have also been bitten by the bug – Matthew Lintz appeared in *H2: Halloween 2*, Macsen Lintz has just made his acting debut as Owen Wilson's son in *Hall Pass* and Madison Lintz appeared in *The Walking Dead*. *The Hunger Games* is Mackenzie's first film, and we think she's one to watch!

Samuel Tan is a newcomer, but has already appeared in Far East Movement's 'Rocketeer' music video, and he does some stunt work. He's also going to appear in the new MTV horror-comedy, *Death Valley*!

Tribute Tweet:

@mackenzielintz "#TheHungerGames. A story for few. A world for most. Happy Hunger Games and May the odds be ever in you favor..."

The industry for District 9 is unknown. It is mentioned that District 9 has many factories, but we don't know what they produce.

District 10 produces livestock, which is an important role. The people of the Capitol love to consume mountains of meat, cream and butter.

"I lost my bread during the struggle with the boy from District 9…"
Katniss

DISTRICT 9 TRIBUTES:

The female Tribute from District 9 is only in the Games for one day.

Katniss and the male Tribute have a close encounter at the Cornucopia – they both run for and wrestle over the same backpack – before he is caught by Clove.

PLAYED BY: **Annie Thurman** is fairly new to Hollywood. Her first role was in another post-apocalyptic film, *Falls The Shadow*, so she'll have plenty of experience fighting for her life on camera!

Newbie **Imanol Yepez-Frias** plays the District 9 male Tribute. We don't know much about him, but we do know that we can't wait to see him onscreen!

DID YOU KNOW? Annie verified her official Twitter account by writing it down and posting an adorable pic of her holding it up for all her adoring fans to see. We like her style!

Tribute Tweet:
@Annirthurman
"#ThingsIDidOverTheSummer filmed #TheHungerGames"

DID YOU KNOW? Dakota's primary passion is music and she loves to sing. Check out her videos on YouTube – this girl is good!

DISTRICT 10 TRIBUTES:

The female Tribute is only in the Games for one day.

The male Tribute has a crippled foot and walks with a limp. When watching him during the pre-Games interviews, Katniss describes him as being very quiet and shy. He leaves the Games on the morning that Katniss blows up the Career pack's supplies.

Tribute Tweet:
@DakotaBHood "I miss my HG family so much #truefriends"

PLAYED BY: **Dakota Hood** is another movie newcomer. Before she landed her break-through role as District 10's female Tribute in *The Hunger Games*, her only part was in *Scripture Cake: A Southern Cuisine Movie* which was filmed back in 2007.

Jeremy Marinas is a super-strong stunt performer and he has worked on both *The Green Hornet* and the upcoming *Sherlock Holmes* sequel – wow, we're sure those stuntman skills will give him an advantage when he's acting out the Arena scenes!

DID YOU KNOW? Jeremy also appeared as a dancer in Justin Bieber: Never Say Never!

DISTRICTS 11 AND 12

District 11 specialises in agriculture, and has many orchards. Discipline is severe in District 11, but at harvest time, children skip school to help.

District 12, which specializes in coal mining, is one of the poorest districts in Panem and many people suffer from starvation. It is surrounded by a high electric fence, which supposedly remains active 24/7, but Katniss knows this is false!

"It's just ... if we didn't win ... I wanted Thresh to. Because he let me go. And because of Rue."
— **Katniss**

DISTRICT 11 TRIBUTES:

Because of her age and size, Rue reminds Katniss of Prim. Small and birdlike, Rue is quick and quiet and able to leap between trees. She becomes allies with Katniss, but is later caught in a net by Marvel.

Thresh is six and a half feet tall and built like an ox. He refuses to join the Careers and makes himself scarce, surviving in the fields beyond the Cornucopia. Thresh leaves the Games during a thunderstorm. Katniss thinks they would have been friends back home.

PLAYED BY: **Amandla Stenberg** was born on 23rd October, 1998, to an African-American mother and a Danish father. She has been modelling for companies like Disney since the age of four and her first feature film was *Columbiana*. Amandla, which means "power" in Zulu, is also a great musician – she can play the violin, drums and guitar and has even performed at the Hard Rock Café and the House of Blues.

Dayo Okeniyi was raised in Lagos, Nigeria, before his family moved to the USA. His full name is pronounced 'Die-O Okay-ni-yii' and his full first name, Oladayo, means "Our wealth has become joy". Dayo began acting at a young age and then returned to it after graduating from college.

He's an amazing actor and we're definitely Team Thresh!

Tribute Tweet:

@amandlastenberg
"Hunger Games fans are the best! Thanks for all your support!"

DID YOU KNOW? Amandla's name is also inspired by an album by jazz musician, Miles Davies.

Tribute Tweet:

@DayoOkeniyi "Last day on set was Sooo bitter sweet! Best summer of my life Hands Down thanks to @JackQuaid92 @alexanderludwig @jermkill @Mark_Reardon"

DISTRICT 12 TRIBUTES:

In the Games, Katniss, or Catnip to her friend Gale, almost dies of dehydration, gets caught in a fireball attack and is chased by the Careers. But cool and clever Katniss, who is handy with a bow and arrows, outsmarts her fellow Tributes at every turn. When she hears that two Tributes from the same District can win, she races to find Peeta. He is wounded, but Katniss wins medicine to cure the infection. After another rule change, Katniss and Peeta threaten to both eat poisonous Nightlock berries, before they are announced joint winners of the 74th Hunger Games!

Peeta, who has beautiful blue eyes, is the noblest Tribute by far! From the moment he is picked at the Reaping, 'the boy with the bread' does everything he can to help Katniss. First, he announces to the whole of Panem that he's in love with her, then he teams up with the Careers in order to protect her from them. Finally, Peeta insists that Katniss must win, because he cannot live without her!

PLAYED BY: Jennifer Lawrence and **Josh Hutcherson**.

DID YOU KNOW? Josh stars in Red Dawn *opposite* Chris Hemsworth, Liam's brother!

DID YOU KNOW? Jennifer was a cheerleader for six years and is very competitive. So she's perfect to play Katniss in the ultimate competition, The Hunger Games!

A NUMBERS GAME

Here's a quiz with a difference: all the answers are numbers. Start counting!

1 How old is Katniss Everdeen?

2 How many loaves of bread did Peeta throw to Katniss, many years ago?

3 How old were Gale and Katniss when they first met?

4 How many siblings does Gale have?

5 How many pets does Prim have?

6 The population of Panem is around . . .

7 How many Districts were there originally in Panem?

8 How many Districts are known to still exist?

9 Which District produces lumber for the Capitol?

10 How many Tributes usually take part in the Games each year?

11 Before Katniss and Peeta, how many Tributes from District 12 had won the Games?

12 How many times was Prim's name down in the Reaping?

13 At what age do children start taking part in the Reaping?

14 Which Games did Katniss and Peeta take part in?

15 Which Games did Haymitch take part in?

16 How many training points did these Tributes get:
      Thresh?
      Peeta?
      Rue?
      Cato?
      Katniss?

17 How many people are there in Katniss's prep team?

18 For how many seconds must the Tributes stand on their metal circles, before the Games begin?

19 How many wolf-like muttations attacked Katniss, Peeta and Cato?

THE CAPITOL

The Capitol is the heart of Panem. It is the most powerful place in the country and controls all the districts. As Katniss learns when she goes there after the Reaping, life in the Capitol is worlds away from the poverty of District 12.

When Panem was first formed, the Capitol was built in what used to be the Rockies, so it is protected by mountains. It was this amazing advantage that allowed them to win the war in the Dark Days. Except for the Tributes who are picked for the Games, no one from the Districts is ever permitted to visit the Capitol, even though they are connected by super-fast train lines that go at 250 miles an hour.

Everything is large and luxurious in the Capitol. The people are incredibly wealthy and don't work anywhere near as hard as the citizens of the Districts. They love colours that are bold, bright and garish. Their fashion is fabulously crazy, with dyed skin and hair, wacky wigs, impractical clothes and all kinds of accessories. They speak in an affected, high-pitched accent and have silly, frivolous names. They have plastic surgery to change their appearance and keep themselves looking younger, they get tattoos and they even implant gems into their skin!

One of the only things to impress Katniss about the Capitol is the food, which is rich and plentiful. She has never seen anything like it and can't get enough of the stews and soups, the fresh fruit, rich sauces, cakes and hot chocolate. It's sumptuous and beautifully prepared and is the complete opposite of the simple fare she's used to back home.

DID YOU KNOW?
The names of many Capitol citizens appear to have been taken from ancient Rome and ancient Greece!

"The cameras haven't lied about the grandeur. If anything, they have not quite captured the magnificence of the glistening buildings in a rainbow of hues that tower into the air, the shiny cars that roll down the wide paved street, the oddly dressed people with bizarre hair and painted faces who have never missed a meal."
Katniss

FIND THE FOOD

They're not called *The Hunger Games* for nothing - Katniss and the other citizens of District 12 are always trying to find food to keep them and their families alive. Now it's your turn! Try to find all the food and drink in this wordsearch . . .

I	D	T	E	A	P	P	L	E	O	D	A	W	T
R	A	W	B	O	N	R	A	M	B	R	O	T	H
T	N	H	E	A	T	I	S	L	O	V	G	E	O
H	D	B	R	E	A	D	P	P	I	N	R	E	T
S	E	S	R	G	R	A	I	N	B	M	O	G	C
A	L	O	I	U	A	N	D	H	L	E	O	R	H
O	I	H	E	F	B	D	L	I	A	M	S	G	O
R	O	D	S	V	B	W	H	E	M	Y	L	S	C
A	N	Y	Z	S	I	O	G	R	B	E	I	K	O
N	G	D	K	A	T	N	I	S	S	V	N	X	L
G	L	Y	A	F	T	Y	J	A	T	D	G	I	A
E	R	G	O	A	T	S	C	H	E	E	S	E	T
W	A	T	E	R	B	U	Y	B	W	I	B	P	E

Lamb stew
Bread
Broth
Rabbit
Katniss
Goat's cheese
Berries
Dandelion
Hot chocolate
Grain
Groosling
Water
Orange
Apple

DID YOU KNOW? Katniss is named after a plant with an edible root, a bit like a potato. The plant has a flower with three white petals.

MEN OF THE CAPITOL

The Capitol is full of powerful men and women, who hold Katniss's fate in their hands . . .

PRESIDENT SNOW

As the head of the Capitol and the twelve Districts, President Snow is the most important man in the whole of Panem. He has been in charge for over 25 years and is a ruthless leader, concerned only with keeping control of his citizens and not at all interested in the wellbeing of the people.

As Katniss quickly comes to realize, he is a deeply dangerous man. When he steps forward to crown Katniss and Peeta victors of the 74th Hunger Games, his eyes are cold, unforgiving and snake-like. President Snow doesn't like what has happened in the Games this year.

Katniss knows that all the power lies with him, that he makes every decision – if he decides he doesn't believe that she loves Peeta, then she might not get to go home to District 12 after the Games and her family and friends will also be in grave danger . . .

DONALD SUTHERLAND

President Snow is all about power and we think veteran actor, Donald Sutherland, is the perfect choice for this pivotal role. He has played many chilling villains and strong, powerful men in the past!

Born on 17 July, 1935, in Canada, Donald has been a Hollywood star for over 50 years and has played more than a hundred parts. From *Pride and Prejudice* and *Cold Mountain* to *Buffy the Vampire Slayer* and *The Italian Job*, he is fantastic in any film genre. Donald has also starred in *The Simpsons*, appearing as has his famous actor son, Kiefer Sutherland. We're so excited to see what Sutherland Senior will be like as scary President Snow!

> *"Occasionally I catch a glimpse of Haymitch, which is reassuring, or President Snow, which is terrifying."*
>
> **Katniss**

DID YOU KNOW?
Donald has played a president before, but in rather a different role. He was the voice of President Stone in the animation Astro Boy!

CAESAR FLICKERMAN

Caesar Flickerman has hosted the Hunger Games interviews for over forty years, though, like many people in the Capitol, he doesn't look like it! He wears white make-up and a blue suit, and whilst his hairstyle doesn't change, his hair colour does. He is friendly and helps the Tributes along, encouraging them to give the audience a good show.

STANLEY TUCCI

Stanley Tucci is just perfect for the flamboyant role of Caesar Flickerman. He's played the part of a total fashionista in *The Devil Wears Prada*, so we know he has the style that is essential for Casear. He is also well known for his chameleon-like ability to change his voice, hair and appearances for his roles, which will be ideal for someone from the Capitol.

Born on 11th November, 1960, Stanley has also starred in *Easy A*, *The Lovely Bones*, and *Captain America*, as well as working as a producer, director and writer. He's a multi-talented man!

> "I'll say this for Caesar, he really does his best to make the Tributes shine."
> **Katniss**

DID YOU KNOW? Stanley once co-owned a restaurant. We wonder if it served the lamb stew that Caesar loves so much!

CLAUDIUS TEMPLESMITH

Claudius Templesmith is the announcer of the Hunger Games, the voice the Tributes hear around the Arena. He is also the TV commentator and announces the rule changes, firstly stating that both Tributes from the same District can win, and then telling Katniss and Peeta that one must kill the other.

TOBY JONES

Like Stanley Tucci, British actor Toby Jones has also just appeared in *Captain America*. Not only that, but he also provided the voice of Dobby in the *Harry Potter* films and has appeared in *Doctor Who*!

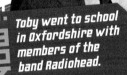

DID YOU KNOW? Toby went to school in Oxfordshire with members of the band Radiohead.

SENECA CRANE

Seneca Crane is the head of the Gamemakers – the people who devise the Arena and control the Hunger Games, as well as giving the Tributes their training scores. Seneca is vital to the success of the Games and so a lot of pressure is riding on him.

WES BENTLEY

Born on 4th September, 1978, dark haired, blue-eyed Wes Bentley made a big impact on Hollywood, shooting to fame as the mysterious bad boy next door in *American Beauty*. This was an impressive feat as he was a relative newcomer and it's been said that he beat 20 young Hollywood actors to the part. Since then he has acted with Heath Ledger in *Four Feathers*, and he plays football in his spare time.

THE DISTRICT 12 AMBASSADOR:
EFFIE TRINKETT

EFFIE TRINKETT

Bright and bubbly, Effie Trinkett is the Capitol's ambassador for District 12. From drawing the names at the Reaping to escorting the Tributes to the Capitol, it's her job to make sure Peeta and Katniss get as much attention and sponsorship as possible.

Like many naïve people raised in the Capitol, Effie views the Games as simply a source of entertainment, so when Katniss volunteers to take Prim's place in the Games, Effie congratulates her excitedly, shouting, 'that's the spirit' and attempts to start a big round of applause. Unfortunately for Effie, the entire District is silent, showing the boldest form of rebellion they can manage, and she is left on the stage clapping and grinning alone.

Prim, proper and pink haired, Effie also represents the wealth, power and frivolity of the Capitol. She is a comical rather than sinister character and, like Katniss, we can't help but warm to her as she does her best to secure sponsors and kick Haymitch into shape.

At first she dislikes her job, determined to be promoted to a better, wealthier District. But as time goes by, Effie grows fond of her District 12 Tributes and when it's time to say goodbye, she tearfully wishes Katniss and Peeta good luck, thanking them for being the best Tributes she has ever worked with.

"It's their job to pay attention to you. And just because you come from District Twelve is no excuse to ignore you."

Effie

"She's so suited to me. She's funny, she's a little comic relief, she's a little kooky, she's a little dark."
Elizabeth Banks

ELIZABETH BANKS

Elizabeth Banks is a terrifically talented actress who has starred in many movies, including all three *Spider-Man* films, *Seabiscuit*, *Catch Me If You Can* and *Role Models*. You may also recognise her as Dr. Kim Briggs in *Scrubs* and, most recently, as Avery Jessup in *30 Rock*.

Back in 2003, Banks married sportswriter and producer Max Handelman, who had been her boyfriend since she met him on her first day at college, in 1992. So sweet! They had their son, Felix, in March 2011 and amazingly, Elizabeth returned to work just two months after giving birth in order to start shooting *The Hunger Games*!

As a huge fan of the books, when Elizabeth heard that *The Hunger Games* was being made into a film, she told the Head of Production at Lionsgate that she would "pay to be Effie". And when she found out that Gary Ross, the director she'd worked with on *Seabiscuit*, was directing the film, she contacted him and said: "I want to be Effie . . . if you want to make life easy, I'm here."

Thankfully, he agreed! Elizabeth is perfect for the part, as she seems just as determined and enthusiastic as Effie is. We can't wait to see her in that fabulous pink wig!

"I read the first one and I was like, 'Oh my God!' I devoured it in, like, five hours... And then I immediately got on the list to get *Catching Fire* and then pre-ordered *Mockingjay*, like, a month in advance."
Elizabeth Banks

GUESS WHO?

Can you guess which Hunger Games character says what? These are all things they say to Katniss . . .

A "If there's one thing we can't stand, it's a whiner. Grease her down!"

B "Don't go. Sing."

C "Got it, sweetheart?"

D "And may the odds be ever in your favor!"

E "Think hard about not showing up. For some of you this will be your last chance."

F "Sorry, we're out of time. Best of luck Katniss Everdeen, Tribute from District Twelve."

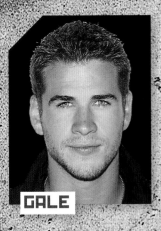

GALE

CLAUDIUS

EFFIE

HAYMITCH

CINNA

THRESH

G "You and I, we could make it."

H "I just want you to come home."

I "Just this one time, I let you go."

J "Remember, they already love you. Just be yourself."

K "Shoot me and he goes down with me."

L "I knew – just like your mother – I was a goner."

M "Forget it, District Twelve. We're going to kill you."

CAESAR

RUE

FLAVIUS

CATO

CLOVE

PRIM

PEETA

THE STYLIST: CINNA

Having the perfect look is a big part of winning the Hunger Games. Not only that, but the people of the Capitol are obsessed with crazy fashions and spend lots of time and money on their looks. So the fashion gurus are at the heart of the Games!

CINNA

Katniss's stylist, Cinna, is a newcomer to the Games and asked for District 12 especially. Cinna doesn't buy into the fashions of the Capitol – he simply wears black, with gold eyeliner. He doesn't speak in the Capitol's high-pitched accent, either.

As Katniss's stylist, Cinna is vital to her success, and he helps create a powerful image for her from the very beginning. Tributes from District 12 usually get dull, coal-related outfits, but Cinna and Peeta's stylist, Portia, put Katniss and Peeta into unitards with capes that have real flames. From that moment on, Katniss is transformed into "The Girl who was on Fire."

Cinna cleverly understands how to use clothes and style to manipulate the audience, and when it becomes vital for Katniss to look as lovelorn and innocent as possible, Cinna can be relied on to deliver the goods.

LENNY KRAVITZ

Lenny Kravitz is pretty new to acting but he's no stranger to showbusiness. Lenny attended Beverley Hills High School, where other former pupils include Angelina Jolie, Leighton Meester and David Schwimmer. He started his musical career performing under the name Romeo Blue and released his debut album in 1989. Since then has had several number 1 hits across the world and has won seven Grammy Awards.

Acting is in Lenny's genes though, as his mother was an actress and his father a television producer. After a cameo in *Zoolander*, Lenny got more acting work, including a role in the movie *Precious*. Lenny's daughter Zoe has got the acting bug too, appearing in *X-Men: First Class* alongside Jennifer Lawrence. Lenny said, "She spent a lot of time at my house in Paris when she was filming. It was fun. They were filming in Pinewood and Zoe and her friends liked to come over. About six of them, usually, and we'd cook for them. And now I'm doing a movie with Jennifer, which is kind of weird."

Lucky Lenny didn't even have to audition for the role, and we agree with the Producers that he'll make the perfect Cinna. He went straight out and read the books, and became hooked on them like a true HG fan. He's as thrilled as we are about the film!

"I'm really excited to be playing Cinna. Reading the book, I'm seeing everything – the Capitol, the Arena, all this stuff. This world is going to be incredible."
Lenny Kravitz

THE PREP TEAM

Cinna has three assistants to help him style Katniss. They are true Capitol citizens and Katniss finds their perspective on the Games difficult to handle. They don't have any understanding of what Katniss's real life is like, but she eventually comes to realise that they do care for her and genuinely want her to succeed.

"They are truly thrilled to see me and I'm happy to see them, too, although not like I was to see Cinna."

Katniss

PORTIA

Portia is Peeta's stylist, and she works closely with Cinna to make sure her outfits for Peeta match Katniss's in their effectiveness.

LATARSHA ROSE

Latarsha has had parts in *All My Children*, *CSI: Miami*, and *Law & Order*. We can't wait to see her glamming up Peeta!

DID YOU KNOW? Lenny Kravitz once provided the voice of a newborn baby on The Rugrats Movie!

VENIA

Venia has aqua hair and gold tattoos above her eyebrows.

KIMIKO GELMAN

Born on 20th February, 1966, Kimiko has had parts in a number of TV shows including *CSI: Miami*, *The West Wing*, *Beverly Hills 90210* and *Zoey 101*. We're looking forward to seeing her fabulous eyebrows in *The Hunger Games*!

"Of all the people I've met since I've left home, Cinna is by far my favourite."

Katniss

OCTAVIA

Octavia is plump and is dyed green all over.

BROOKE BUNDY

Brooke, a relative newcomer to acting, plays Octavia. We bet she's excited to get dressed up as wonderfully wacky Octavia!

DID YOU KNOW? Nelson Ascensio is a twin, just like Willow Shields!

FLAVIUS

Flavius has hair in orange corkscrew curls and wears purple lipstick.

NELSON ASCENCIO

Nelson was born in Cuba on 30th August, 1964, and studied acting at the American Academy of Dramatic Arts and at HB Studios in Greenwich Village. He has done stand-up comedy as well as improvisation, so he'll be a hoot as Flavius!

TEST YOUR HUNGER GAMES KNOWLEDGE!

It's time to see how much you know about the world of the Hunger Games. Take this quick quiz to find out!

1 Who is the host of the Hunger Games?

2 Gale had five entries in the Reaping when he was just twelve years old. True or false?

3 Peeta's father brings Katniss a present before she leaves for the Capitol. What is it?

4 What colour dress does Katniss wear to the Reaping?

5 What is Gale's nickname for Katniss?

6 Haymitch won the 50th Hunger Games. This special Games is also known as what?

7 What is the name of Prim's cat?

8 How many Tributes die on the first day?

9   Which Tribute is Katniss's first direct kill?

10   When Katniss was young, Peeta saved her from starvation. What flower does Katniss see afterwards that gives her hope?

11   Peeta has two brothers. True or false?

12   What is the name of the boy from District 2?

13   What place does Foxface come in the Games?

14   How many signal fires should Rue have set?

15   How did Katniss's father die?

16   Shortly after Rue's death, Katniss receives a gift. What is it?

17   What is the name of Peeta's stylist?

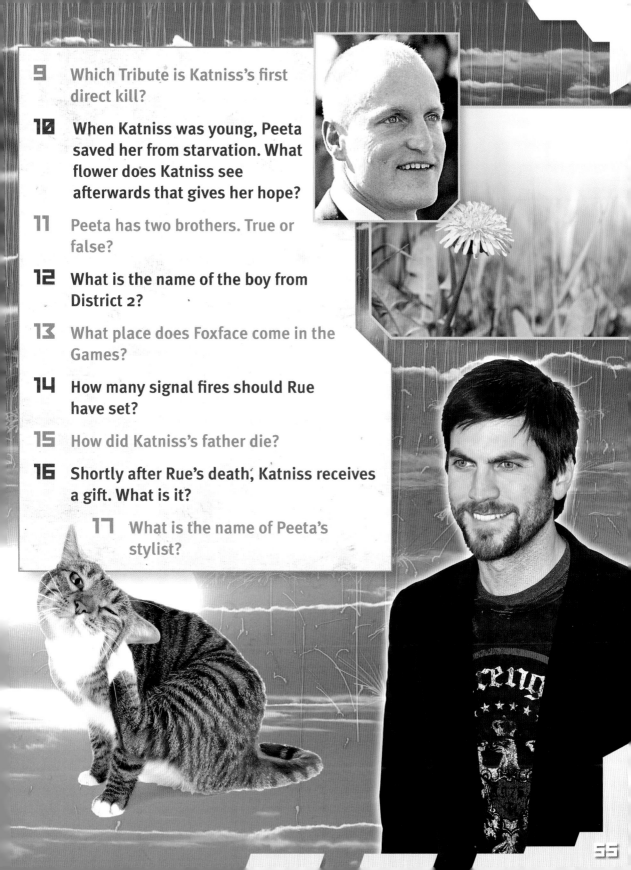

18 What does Katniss trick Peeta into drinking, so that she can go to the feast to get the medicine he needs?

19 Who designs and controls the Hunger Games and can intervene at any moment, to make things more interesting?

20 What is the name of the wealthiest part of Panem?

21 Historically 'the uprising of the 13 Districts' against the Capitol is also referred to as what?

22 Cinna doesn't have a Capitol accent or wear bizarre clothes. What is his only Capitol feature?

23 What is Peeta's secret weapon in the Arena?

24 In the caves, Katniss tells Peeta and Panem the story of when . . .

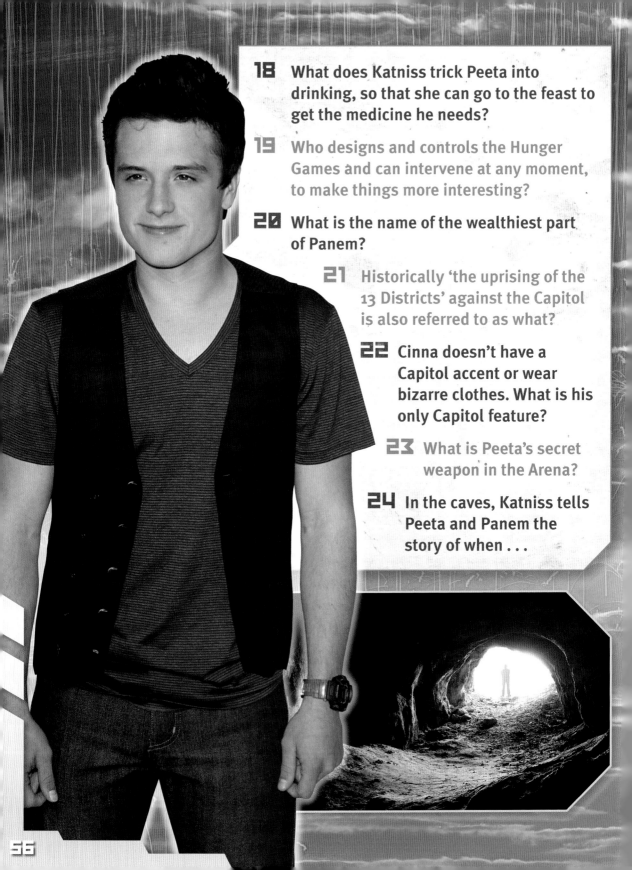

A TO Z OF THE HUNGER GAMES

A **AVOX** An Avox is a person who has been punished for rebelling against the Capitol, rendered unable to speak.

B **BOW AND ARROWS** Katniss's weapon of choice. Her father taught her to shoot and after years of practise, she has an amazing aim.

C **CAPITOL** The Capitol is the wealthiest place in Panem. It's also a dictatorship, run by President Snow.

D **DISTRICTS** There were once thirteen Districts in Panem, each with a different industry, until District 13 was destroyed. District 12 is Katniss, Gale and Peeta's home, where coal is mined.

E **EFFIE TRINKET** Effie is the ambassador for District 12, looking after Katniss and Peeta when they're picked for the 74th Hunger Games.

F **FEAST** When the audience isn't seeing enough action, the Gamemakers set up a feast, to lure the Tributes in and force them to fight.

G **GARY ROSS** Gary is the Director of *The Hunger Games* film.

H **HAYMITCH ABERNATHY** As the winner of the 50th Hunger Games, Haymitch must now act as mentor for the two Tributes from District 12.

I **INTERVENTION** From the fireballs set off by the Gamemakers to the food and medicine sent by the sponsors, there is always some form of intervention to hinder or help the Tributes.

J **JABBERJAYS** These birds were created by the Capitol to record rebels' conversations. After this plan was foiled and then abandoned, male jabberjays bred with female mockingbirds to create mockingjays, which became Katniss's symbol.

K **KATNISS EVERDEEN** The heroine of *The Hunger Games*, Katniss is the female Tribute from District 12 who goes on to become joint winner with her fellow D12 Tribute, Peeta.

L **LAMB STEW** This scrumptious stew quickly becomes Katniss's favourite food from the Capitol.

M **MUTTATIONS** The Capitol created many creatures that are extra-vicious versions of their original form. Katniss encounters both tracker jackers and wolf-like beasts in the Arena.

N **NIGHTLOCK BERRIES** These are the poisonous berries that Katniss uses to allow both her and Peeta to win. Foxface died after consuming them.

O **OCTAVIA** Katniss has a stylist, Cinna, and a prep team to ensure she looks her best before the Hunger Games. Octavia is a member of the prep team and Katniss comes to like her very much.

P **PEETA MELARK** Katniss thinks of Peeta, her fellow District 12 Tribute, as 'the boy with the bread'. He does everything he can to protect her during their time in the Games.

Q **QUARTER QUELL** Every 25 years, the Hunger Games has a Quarter Quell, which means there will be an added tortuous twist. Next year's Games will be the 75th, so it will be a Quarter Quell.

R **REAPING** The residents of each District gather together for the Reaping, where the names of the two Tributes who will take part in the Games are announced.

S **SUZANNE COLLINS** Suzanne is the amazing author of *The Hunger Games*, the trilogy of books that have gained fans from around the world.

T **TRIBUTES** Two Tributes, one male and one female, are picked from each District every year, to take part in the Hunger Games.

U **UNDERSEE** The Mayor of District 12's last name is Undersee. His daughter is Madge, who becomes friends with Katniss and gives her the mockingjay pin as a gift before the Games.

V **VICTORS' VILLAGE** This is where the winning Tribute lives after surviving the Games. Before Katniss and Peeta won, Haymitch was the only person living in District 12's Victor's Village.

W **WINNER** Usually, there can only be one winner of the Games. Katniss and Peeta are the only exceptions to this rule, much to President Snow's annoyance.

X **X MARKS THE SPOT** Peeta makes an X on Cato's hand, as a target for Katniss to shoot at. This saves Peeta's life.

Y **YIPPING** The wolf-like muttations that attack Katniss, Peeta and Cato at the Cornucopia make a terrifying, high-pitched noise to communicate with each other.

Z **ZANE** Debra Zane is the Casting Director for *The Hunger Games*. We think she chose the perfect cast for this fantastic film!

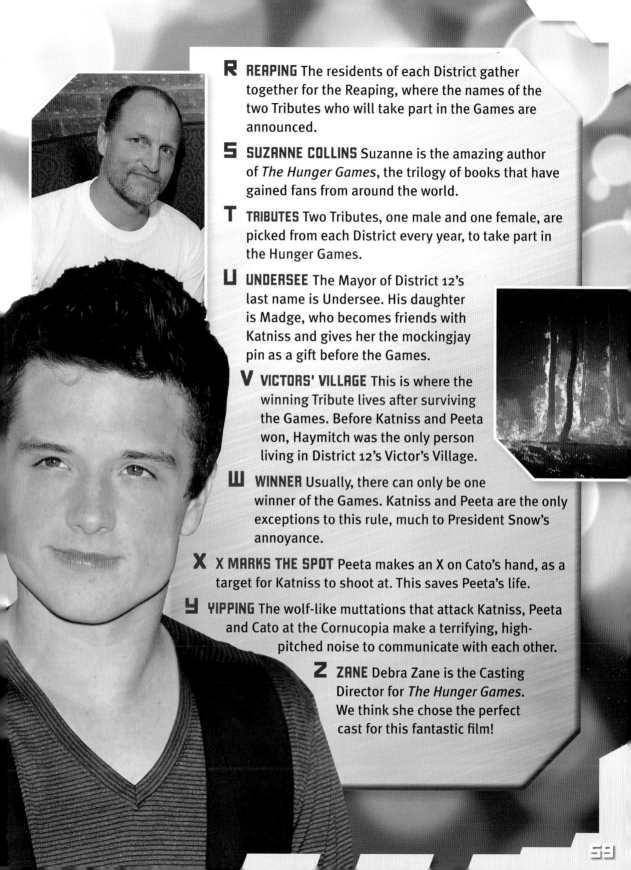

BUZZ ABOUT THE NEXT FILM

Frustrated because you have to wait AGES for your next Hunger Games *fix? Well, this should cheer you up: Lionsgate have already announced a release date for the second movie.* Catching Fire *should hit our screens on 22nd November, 2013. Hurrah!*

SPOILER ALERT!

So, what can we expect from *Catching Fire*?

Well, in the book, Katniss and Peeta will finally return home to their families, after winning the 74th Hunger Games. Surely, as joint winners, they will be living in the Victors Village, together? This could be a little awkward, seeing as they aren't speaking! Will Peeta forgive Katniss for pretending to love him in order to win? How will Gale react when the star-crossed lovers return, after having watched their televised romance? And, more importantly, will Katniss decide to admit to her feelings for Peeta or instead explore her relationship with Gale? The suspense is killing us!

Next year is the 75th Hunger Games and it's not just any Games, it's a Quarter Quell. Quarter Quells happen every twenty-five years and, as they mark the anniversary of the Districts' defeat by the Capitol, they are always especially brutal. So, expect twists, turns and a truly terrifying Games. Will Katniss and Peeta be forced to mentor the two new Tributes from their District, or will something even more terrible take place?

Only one thing is certain: Since Katniss instigated the incident with the Nightlock berries – forcing the Gamemakers to allow both her and Peeta to win the Games – she is viewed by certain people as the one to blame for making the Capitol look stupid. President Snow is furious and we, along with Katniss, must get ready for his ruthless revenge.

It sounds like *Catching Fire* will be even more dramatic than *The Hunger Games*. And we can't wait . . .

PAGE 42

A NUMBERS GAME

1) 16
2) 2
3) 14 and 12
4) 3
5) 2
6) 8000
7) 13
8) 12
9) 7
10) 24
11) 2
12) 1
13) 12
14) 74th
15) 50th
16) Thresh: 10, Peeta: 8, Rue: 7, Cato: 10, Katniss: 11
17) 3
18) 60
19) 21

PAGE 50

GUESS WHO?

a) Flavius
b) Rue
c) Haymitch
d) Effie
e) Claudius
f) Caesar
g) Gale
h) Prim
i) Thresh
j) Cinna
k) Cato
l) Peeta
m) Clove

PAGE 54

TEST YOUR HUNGER GAMES KNOWLEDGE!

1) Caesar Flickerman
2) False, he had six
3) Cookies

4) Blue
5) Catnip
6) A Quarter Quell
7) Buttercup
8) 11
9) The male Tribute from District 1
10) Dandelion
11) True
12) Cato
13) 4th place
14) 3
15) In a mining accident
16) Bread from District 11
17) Portia
18) Sleep syrup
19) The Gamemakers
20) The Capitol
21) The Dark Days
22) Gold eyeliner
23) Camouflage
24) She brought Prim a goat

PAGE 45 FIND THE FOOD

I	D	T	E	A	P	P	L	E	O	D	A	W	T
R	A	W	B	O	N	R	A	M	B	R	O	T	H
T	N	H	E	A	T	I	S	L	O	V	G	E	O
H	D	B	R	E	A	D	P	P	I	N	R	E	T
S	E	S	R	G	R	A	I	N	B	M	O	G	C
A	L	O	I	U	A	N	D	H	L	E	O	R	H
O	I	H	E	F	B	D	L	I	A	M	S	G	O
R	O	D	S	V	B	W	H	E	M	Y	L	S	C
A	N	Y	Z	S	I	O	G	R	B	E	I	K	O
N	G	D	K	A	T	N	I	S	S	V	N	X	O
G	L	Y	A	F	T	Y	J	A	T	D	G	I	A
E	R	G	O	A	T	S	C	H	E	E	S	E	T
W	A	T	E	R	B	U	Y	B	W	I	B	P	E